MW00562779

# LABELS
## and
# BOTTLES
## OF THE CRAFT SPIRITS INDUSTRY

Bill Owens
American Distilling Institute

Introduction by Nancy Fraley, *Director of Research, American Distilling Institute*
Andrew Faulkner, *Photography*
Gail Sands, Pica Graphics, *Design*

©2011
White Mule Press
distilling.com

*Hand distilled*

*Hand distilled*

*Hand distilled*

WESTFORD HILL DISTILLERS
Series No. 5
Bottle No. 246

Kirsch
*Eau~de~vie*

WESTFORD HILL DISTILLERS
Series No. 5
Bottle No. 624

Fraise
*Eau~de~vie*
STRAWBERRY BRANDY
ALC. 40% BY VOL

WESTFORD HILL DISTILLERS
Series No. 6
Bottle No. 228

Pear William
*Eau~de~vie*
PEAR BRANDY
ALC. 40% BY VOL

**WESTFORD HILLS DISTILLERY**

# INTRODUCTION

There is nothing that outwardly conveys the identity of a craft distilled spirit more than its label. It is the calling card that gives the consumer a hint about what is inside the bottle. And it speaks volumes about the individuality of the distillery, the distiller who made it, and why. That is why it carries such weight.

Federal law mandates that all labels for domestically produced distilled spirits have six basic elements: brand name, alcohol content, net contents, class and type designation, name and address of the distiller or bottler, and the government warning statement. While certain aspects of the mandatory label information for both domestic and imported distillates differ according to the class and type of spirit, all labels must meet certain requirements regarding font size and legibility.

It is precisely in the frontier between strict federal legal requirements and the limits of tired, traditional post-Prohibition labels where an unprecedented creativity in label design is now occurring. Just as we are seeing the new breed of craft distillers push all known boundaries of spirits production through the creation of new recipes, types and categories of products, there is also a renaissance that is occurring within the design of the labels themselves.

Each label, coupled with the shape of the bottle, conveys an important artistic message that the distillery wishes to send to the potential consumer about the liquid inside. Some labels are made to be as stark and minimalist as possible, such as the thin white paper band with typewriter written wording found on the King's County Distillery moonshine corn whiskey pocket-sized flask. Other labels, such as the elegant etchings used for Huber Starlight Distillery's aged brandy, well compliment the graceful curves of the bottle and offer the drinker a glimpse into the years of hard work it took to produce what is inside. St. George Spirits' Hangar One vodka label is elemental in design, with a band of single color wrapping around the bottle, while the distinctive funny-shaped, squat bottles with rustic brown or cream paper identify Tuthilltown Distillery's line of whiskeys. Each of these labels, as well as all the rest that are included in this book, represent a distillery's highest goals and aspirations as to who they are and what audience they intend to reach.

It is quite an exciting time in the distilled spirits industry as there are now well over 324 craft distilleries in the United States. As more distilleries are added to that list, we will continue to see a surge in creativity in both the products produced and the labels designed to grace the front of each bottle. This book is an attempt to capture some of that innovation and to celebrate it. While you are perusing through the label designs, I invite you to pour a glass of your favorite craft-made whiskey, brandy or rum. Join in the celebration of the craft distilling and label design revolution!

—*Nancy Fraley*
*Director of Research, American Distilling Institute*

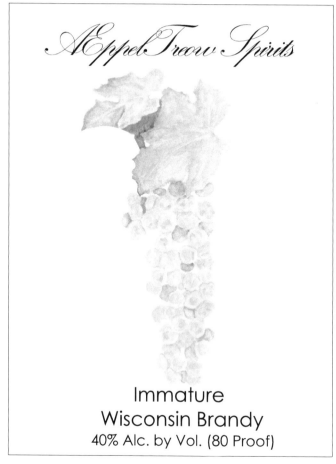

### Immature
### Wisconsin Brandy
40% Alc. by Vol. (80 Proof)

**AEPPLETREOW DISTILLEY**

*The labels and bottles in this book do not represent the actual color or size of the originals.*

*In the production of the book we ran into a number of problems in the classification of craft spirits. For example, the brandy chapter contains labels of products made from grapes and fruit. In the whiskey chapter there are labels from malt, corn rye and wheat as defined in the TTB...CFR 5.22. Moonshine is not defined by TTB so the labels and bottles included here reflect the history of moonshine. Most shines are made with unaged corn whiskey, but in this book you will find shines made with buckwheat, rye, etc. Reality is, moonshine is often made from anything that ferments (like donuts).*

*The design of the labels in this book reflect the spirit of a new generation of craft distillers. Enjoy this book as a look at the diversity and creativity in a revival of the craft of distillation—not as a definition of each spirit category.*

*A best effort was made to contact all distillers for their labels.*

# CONTENTS

# ABSINTHE

LEOPOLD BROS.

Absinthe Verte

Grape spirits distilled
with herbs, with
natural flavors added

750 ML. 65% ALC BY VOL BATCH LD

ABSINTHE VERTE

ST. GEORGE

FINE BRANDY WITH THE
CHOICEST HERBS

OUR FINE ABSINTHE VERTE IS THE RE
OF YEARS OF PATIENT EXPERIMEN
IN HERBAL DISTILLATION. ITS COM
COMES FROM THE USE OF FINE BR
STAR ANISE, MINT, WORMWOOD,
BALM, HYSSOP, MEADOWSWEET
FENNEL, TARRAGON AND STINGING

Lance C. Winters – Distiller

PRODUCT OF USA

La Sorcière™

ABSINTHE SUPÉRIEURE

BRANDY DISTILLED WITH
HERBS AND WITH HERBS ADDED

750 ml          50% Alc. By Vol.

La Sorcière™

ABSINTHE BLEUE

BRANDY DISTILLED
WITH HERBS

750 ml          50% Alc. By Vol.

DISTILLED & BOTTLED BY
PACIFIC DISTILLERY LLC
WOODINVILLE, WA USA

www.pacificdistillery.com

CAUTION: Pacifique should not be
ignited. In addition to spoiling the
fine nuances of herbal flavor, there
is a risk of accidental fire and injury.

GOVERNMENT WARNING: (1) ACCORDING
TO THE SURGEON GENERAL, WOMEN SHOULD
NOT DRINK ALCOHOLIC BEVERAGES DURING
PREGNANCY BECAUSE OF THE RISK OF BIRTH
DEFECTS. (2) CONSUMPTION OF ALCOHOLIC
BEVERAGES IMPAIRS YOUR ABILITY TO DRIVE A
CAR OR OPERATE MACHINERY, AND MAY
CAUSE HEALTH PROBLEMS.

8 98322 00201 3

MÉTHODE ANCIENNE

# PACIFIQUE

ABSINTHE
VERTE SUPÉRIEURE

GRAIN NEUTRAL SPIRITS DISTILLED
AND INFUSED WITH HERBS AND SPICES

750 ML       62% ALC/VOL (124 PROOF)

Pacifique Absinthe Verte
Supérieure is created using
only the finest hand-
selected whole botanicals
from around the world, and
using only 19th century
artisan distiller techniques.

Pacifique is made in small
batches, by hand, in an
authentic copper alembic
potstill ensuring Old World
artistry and craftsmanship.

Pacifique is distilled in
exact accordance with an
1855 French recipe, and is
crafted with these
traditional botanicals:

Anise, Angelica, Coriander,
Fennel, Hyssop, Melissa,
Grand Wormwood, and
Roman Wormwood.

GREENWAY DISTILLERS

Germain-Robin

AROMATIC BRANDY
DISTILLED WITH HERBS
WITH NATURAL FLAVORS ADDED

ABSINTHE SUPERIEURE

375 ML.                    ALC. 45.15% BY VOL.

# AGAVE

# BRANDY

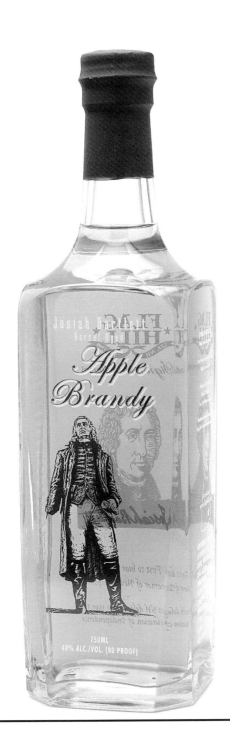

FHF DISTILLERY • VERMONT

# Pomme de Vie™

VERMONT — APPLE BRANDY

ALCOHOL 40% BY VOL.
(80 PROOF) 375 ML

CLEAR CREEK DISTILLERY

MARC, A TRADITIONAL
BRANDY DISTILLED FROM
THE GEWÜRZTRAMINER
GRAPE.

ONLY FROM
GEWÜRZTRAMINER

*Marc*
BRANDY

DISTILLED AND BOTTLED BY
CLEAR CREEK DISTILLERY  PORTLAND, OREGON USA
375ML ALCOHOL 40% BY VOLUME (80 PROOF)

Pot
Distilled

CLEAR CREEK DISTILLERY

# OREGON
# BRANDY

*Traditional brandy pot-distilled from fine Oregon wine*

DISTILLED AND BOTTLED BY
CLEAR CREEK DISTILLERY
PORTLAND, OREGON • PRODUCT OF USA
750 ML • ALC. 42.5% BY VOL. (85 PROOF)

**WILLIAMS PEAR**

**SLIVOVITZ**

## CLEAR CREEK DISTILLERY

PURE FRUIT

BARTLETT PEAR

*Pear Brandy*

ALCOHOL 40%
BY VOLUME
**80** PROOF

DISTILLED AND BOTTLED BY
CLEAR CREEK DISTILLERY
PORTLAND OREGON
PRODUCT OF U.S.A.

750 ml.

## CLEAR CREEK DISTILLERY

*Blue Plum Brandy*

THIS BRANDY IS POT DISTILLED FROM A PURE
FERMENTED MASH OF ITALIAN BLUE PLUMS,
MUCH AS IT HAS BEEN MADE FOR CENTURIES
IN FRANCE WHERE IT IS KNOWN AS Quetsch,
GERMANY AS Zwetschgenwasser, AND IN
MUCH OF EASTERN EUROPE AS Slivovitz.

Distilled and Bottled by Clear Creek Distillery Portland, Oregon Product of U.S.A.
Alcohol 40% by Vol. (80proof) 750ml

Brandy *Peak*

*Spirit*
of

**PEAR**
**BRANDY**

DISTILLED AND BOTTLED BY
BRANDY PEAK DISTILLERY
BROOKINGS, OREGON USA
DSP OR-11

**HEIRLOOM**

Apple brandy aged five
years in French Oak

40% alcohol by volume

Distilled and bottled by
**ST. GEORGE SPIRITS**

BLACK HERON

BRANDY

Distilled from Washington State Wine

40% ALC BY VOL  (80 PROOF)

Distilled and Bottled by
BLACK HERON SPIRITS LLC
West Richland WA 99353
Drink Responsibily
www.blackheronspirits.com

750ML

6 67359 86000 8

GOVERNMENT WARNING: (1) According to the Surgeon General, women should not drink alcoholic beverages during pregnancy beause of the risk of birth defects. (2) Consumption of alcoholic beverages impairs your ability to drive a car or operate machinery, and may cause health problems.

Colorado
GOLD

Less than Two Years Old

BRANDY

40% Alcohol by Volume

YaHaraRay

apple
brandy

MADE

DISTILLED IN MADISON, WI
40% ALC./VOL. 375 ML

APPLEJACK

STARLIGHT

★

DISTILLERY

750 ml-41.5%/Vol

(83 Proof)

GREAT LAKES
DISTILLERY

*Artisan Series*

Pear
Brandy
Eau-de-Vie

*A Product of Wisconsin*

ALC By Volume

GOLDEN

*Apple Brandy*

*Made with Skagit Valley
Jonagold Apples*

**Distilled & Bottled by
Golden NorthWest Distillery, Bow, Washington
Product of USA**

40% ALC/VOL (80 PROOF)          750 ML

'PEAR

SMALL BATCH DISTILLED

HUDSON VALLEY
PEAR BRANDY
375 ML 40% ALC/VOL

LEOPOLD'S

# PISCO *Style*

## AMERICAN BRANDY

Steeped in Chilean tradition, this distinctive spirit is distilled in small hand-hammered copper pot stills from the prized Chilean Muscat grape. Found only in narrow valleys surrounding the Andes Mountains, the lively aroma and delicate finish of the rare Chilean Muscat Grape makes this one of the world's most unique spirits. Its subtlety and complexity make it the perfect cornerstone for the adventurous and refined palate.

750 ML
45% A.B.V.

BATCH NO.
08-01

LEOPOLD BROS.

jack and jenny

kirsch
cherry
brandy

Handmade in small batches
Distilled & Bottled by Peach Street Distillers
Palisade, Colorado
375 ml ALC/VOL 40% (80 PROOF)

jack and jenny

eau-de-vie
apricot
brandy

Handmade in small batches
Distilled & Bottled by Peach Street Distillers
Palisade, Colorado
375 ml ALC/VOL 40% (80 PROOF)

# MOSBY

## PLUM BRANDY
### DAMSON PLUM

Harvested from a small orchard in San Benito County, California, these perfectly ripened plums were artfully fermented and distilled by Bill Mosby under the Rabbinical supervision of Rabbi Yonah Bookstein. This exceptional brandy (Slivovitz) is certified Kosher for Passover L' Mehadrin.

Kosher for Passover
כשר לפסח למהדרין
רב המפשיר רב יונה בוקשטיין

DISTILLED AND BOTTLED BY MOSBY VINTNERS
BUELLTON, CALIFORNIA
ALCOHOL 43.3% BY VOLUME

GOVERNMENT WARNING: (1) ACCORDING TO THE SURGEON GENERAL, WOMEN SHOULD NOT DRINK ALCOHOLIC BEVERAGES DURING PREGNANCY BECAUSE OF THE RISK OF BIRTH DEFECTS. (2) CONSUMPTION OF ALCOHOLIC BEVERAGES IMPAIRS YOUR ABILITY TO DRIVE A CAR OR OPERATE MACHINERY, AND MAY CAUSE HEALTH PROBLEMS.

750ml

# MOSBY

KOSHER

## PLUM BRANDY
### SLIVOVITZ

ALC. 43.3% BY VOL.

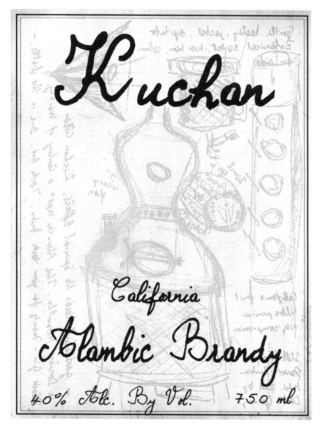

# EAUX DE VIE

CLEAR CREEK
DISTILLERY

EAU DE VIE
OF
DOUGLAS FIR

CALLED EAU DE VIE DE
BOURGEONS DE SAPIN
IN ALSACE

BRANDY
DISTILLED & BOTTLED
BY
CLEAR CREEK
DISTILLERY
IN
PORTLAND
OREGON
U.S.A.

ALCOHOL 47.73% BY VOL.
95.46° PROOF 375 ML

CLEAR CREEK DISTILLERY

Brandy
made from
organically grown
Mirabelle
plums from
King Estate

Eau de Vie
of
Mirabelle

Distilled & Bottled by Clear Creek Distillery

PORTLAND, OR, U.S.A. • 375 ML. • 40% ALC. BY VOL.

CLEAR CREEK

*Eau de Vie de Poire*

To conserve the pear in the bottle, keep it covered by the eau-de-vie. A few particles of the pear may break loose in the brandy. This is normal.

WILLIAMS PEAR BRANDY IS MADE FROM PEARS GROWN IN OUR FAMILY ORCHARDS IN PARKDALE, OREGON. DISTILLED & BOTTLED BY CLEAR CREEK DISTILLERY PORTLAND, OREGON.

BOTTLED AT ALC. 40% BY VOL. (80 PROOF)

PRODUCT OF U.S.A. 750 ML.

CLEAR CREEK

*Eau de Vie de Pomme*

APPLE BRANDY BARREL-AGED
IN LIMOUSIN OAK

DISTILLED AND BOTTLED BY
CLEAR CREEK DISTILLERY  PORTLAND, OREGON
ALCOHOL 40% BY VOL. (80 PROOF) 750 ML

PRODUCT OF U.S.A.

STILLWATER

PETALUMA CALIFORNIA

SPIRITS

# Framboise Eau de Vie

RASPBERRY
BRANDY

MADE IN THE USA

375ML • 40% ALC. BY VOL.
80 PROOF

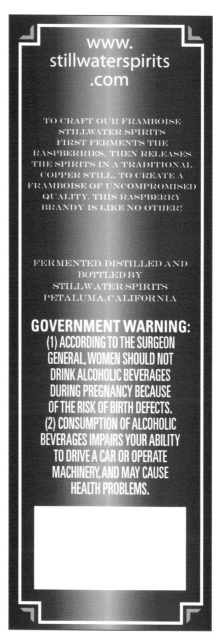

www.
stillwaterspirits
.com

TO CRAFT OUR FRAMBOISE
STILLWATER SPIRITS
FIRST FERMENTS THE
RASPBERRIES, THEN RELEASES
THE SPIRITS IN A TRADITIONAL
COPPER STILL, TO CREATE A
FRAMBOISE OF UNCOMPROMISED
QUALITY. THIS RASPBERRY
BRANDY IS LIKE NO OTHER!

FERMENTED, DISTILLED AND
BOTTLED BY
STILLWATER SPIRITS
PETALUMA, CALIFORNIA

**GOVERNMENT WARNING:**
(1) ACCORDING TO THE SURGEON
GENERAL, WOMEN SHOULD NOT
DRINK ALCOHOLIC BEVERAGES
DURING PREGNANCY BECAUSE
OF THE RISK OF BIRTH DEFECTS.
(2) CONSUMPTION OF ALCOHOLIC
BEVERAGES IMPAIRS YOUR ABILITY
TO DRIVE A CAR OR OPERATE
MACHINERY, AND MAY CAUSE
HEALTH PROBLEMS.

APPLE
EAU DE VIE
APPLE BRANDY

Distilled from
Washington Apples

Distilled and bottled by
San Juan Island Distillery, LLC
Friday Harbor, Washington, USA

375ML        40%ALC/VOL

Old World
Spirits

Eau De Vie
Apricot

Fall 2005
Double Distilled
Charcoal Polished
Sterile Filtered
Alcohol 43% by Vol.
375 ml

AQUA
PERFECTA
CRAFTED BY ST. GEORGE SPIRITS

basil eau de vie
BASIL FLAVORED BRANDY

# GIN

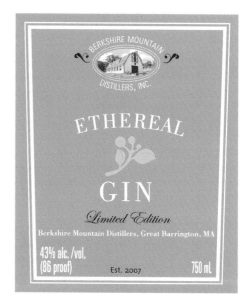

ESTABLISHED 1996

**B**

BENDISTILLERY

CASCADE MOUNTAIN

Hand Crafted American

**Gin**

100% Natural Grain Spirits
Crafted with hand picked wild juniper berries

750 ML

95 PROOF ALCOHOL   47.5% BY VOLUME

BARDENAY

*London Style*

DRY GIN

DISTILLED AND BOTTLED BY
SETTLES KRICK, INC., BOISE, IDAHO

NET CONTENTS      47.1% ALC/VOL
750 ML               94.2 PROOF

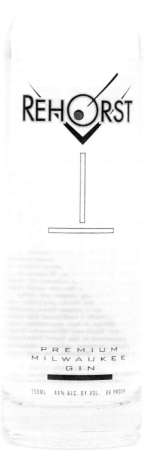

CORIANDRUM SATIVUM ∘ IRIS GERMANICA ∘ JUNIPERUS COMMUNIS ∘ CITRUS SINENSIS ∘ CITRUS LIMON ∘ ELETTARIA CARDAMOMUM ∘ ANGELICA ARCHANGELICA

COLD RIVER®
*Traditional*
GIN

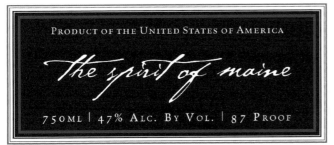

PRODUCT OF THE UNITED STATES OF AMERICA

*the spirit of maine*

750ML | 47% ALC. BY VOL. | 87 PROOF

ORGANIC
NATION
O·N
gin

OREGON'S ORGANIC SPIRIT™

ALC 43% BY VOL (86 PROOF) 750 ML

AVIATION GIN

BATCH DISTILLED

42% ALC/VOL (84 PROOF) 750ML

GOVERNMENT WARNING: (1) ACCORDING TO THE SURGEON GENERAL, WOMEN SHOULD NOT DRINK ALCOHOLIC BEVERAGES DURING PREGNANCY BECAUSE OF THE RISK OF BIRTH DEFECTS. (2) CONSUMPTION OF ALCOHOLIC BEVERAGES IMPAIRS YOUR ABILITY TO DRIVE A CAR OR OPERATE MACHINERY, AND MAY CAUSE HEALTH PROBLEMS.

DISTILLED & BOTTLED BY HOUSE SPIRITS, LLC, PORTLAND, OR

A DARING MIX OF FLORAL, SPICE, CITRUS AND HERB COMPONENTS ARE DISTILLED IN OUR COPPER POT STILL TO PRODUCE A GIN OF BOLD CHARACTER AND REFINED TASTE.

DESIGN: MOTO INTERACTIVE + BRANDING

DISTILLERY № 209

EDGE HILL

DISTILLERY № 209

CORSAIR
Gin
44% ALC/VOL (88 PROOF)

GIN-HEAD STYLE AMERICAN GIN

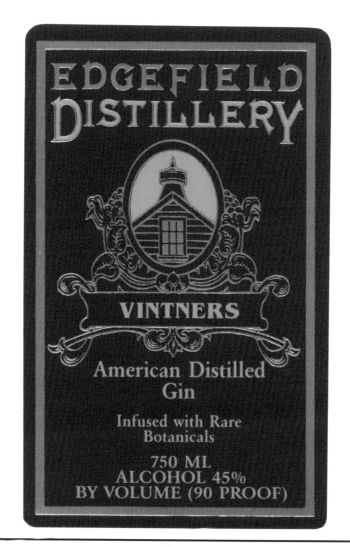

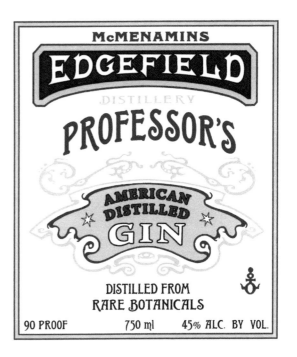

**McMENAMINS**

# EDGEFIELD

DISTILLERY

## PROFESSOR'S

### AMERICAN DISTILLED GIN

DISTILLED FROM
RARE BOTANICALS

90 PROOF          750 ml          45% ALC. BY VOL.

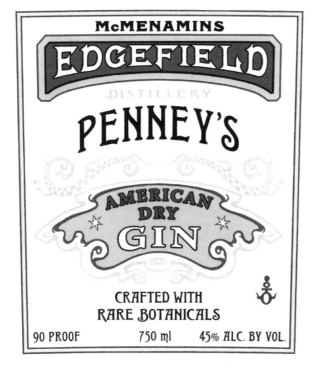

**McMENAMINS**

# EDGEFIELD

DISTILLERY

## PENNEY'S

### AMERICAN DRY GIN

CRAFTED WITH
RARE BOTANICALS

90 PROOF          750 ml          45% ALC. BY VOL.

Tipperary son and language professor John Murphy taught in England and far-flung points of the British Empire before making his way to Portland in 1880. While regarded as one of the most highly educated men on the west coast, Murphy was not without fault. By the early 1900s, "a victim of his own unfortunate habits," the professor was living at the poor farm, now McMenamins Edgefield. A friend remarked, "In his best moments, he was a splendid, honorable and lovable gentleman."

**DISTILLED AND BOTTLED BY**
**EDGEFIELD DISTILLERY**
TROUTDALE, OR 97060
(503) 669-8610

DISTILLED FROM GRAIN

**GOVERNMENT WARNING:**
(1) ACCORDING TO THE SURGEON GENERAL, WOMEN SHOULD NOT DRINK ALCOHOLIC BEVERAGES DURING PREGNANCY BECAUSE OF THE RISK OF BIRTH DEFECTS.
(2) CONSUMPTION OF ALCOHOLIC BEVERAGES IMPAIRS YOUR ABILITY TO DRIVE A CAR OR OPERATE MACHINERY, AND MAY CAUSE HEALTH PROBLEMS.

# PROHIBITION
## GIN

### HANDCRAFTED IN THE HEARTLAND

DISTILLED & BOTTLED IN INDIANA U.S.A.
40% ALC/VOL (80 PROOF) DISTILLED FROM GRAIN

*JR'S SPIRITS* NO.9

*Mean Gin*

*98 Proof*

# RIVER ROSE

### ✦ GIN ✦

750 ML

40% ALC/VOL

**HANDCRAFTED IN IOWA**

**RIVER ROSE HONORS AN ERA** when life along the river was gracious and inspiring. It is handmade in the historic river town of Le Claire, Iowa, along a dramatic bend in the Mississippi where steamboat pilots of old would dock and hire local river pilots to navigate the harrowing rapids ahead. Reflecting that deep respect for local expertise, River Rose is distilled with fresh grains from local farmers, highlighted with the aroma of juniper, citrus, rose petals and homegrown cucumbers. Enjoy River Rose and raise a glass to these legendary navigators.

✦✦

Distilled & Bottled by
## MISSISSIPPI RIVER DISTILLING COMPANY
Le Claire, Iowa

### TheStoryOfRose.com

**GOVERNMENT WARNING:** (1) ACCORDING TO THE SURGEON GENERAL, WOMEN SHOULD NOT DRINK ALCOHOLIC BEVERAGES DURING PREGNANCY BECAUSE OF THE RISK OF BIRTH DEFECTS. (2) CONSUMPTION OF ALCOHOLIC BEVERAGES IMPAIRS YOUR ABILITY TO DRIVE A CAR OR OPERATE MACHINERY, AND MAY CAUSE HEALTH PROBLEMS.

**DISTILLED FROM GRAIN**

**IA REF 5¢**

0  22099  14771  8

## BLADE GIN

Blade(tm) Gin is an ultra-premium, artisanal, California Gin, slowly crafted in small batches on the shores of San Francisco Bay by a family owned artisanal distillery. Blade (tm) Gin bursts with rich, locally sourced herbs and choice California citrus captured by our proprietary three stage extraction process using a custom copper pot still, designed by and manufactured exclusively for our master distiller, Davorin Kuchan. Blade(tm) Gin is the result of years of deep-seated passion for craft distilled gins with an inimitable California twist.

Bold, balanced and dangerously smooth, Blade(tm) Gin will shine in any pre-prohibition cocktail, render an amazing Blade & Tonic and perform like a rock star in a Blade Martini with a lemon and mandarin twist. We hope you will love it as much as we do.

**GOOD STUFF NEEDS**

**NO SPECIAL EFFECTS**

### OLD WORLD SPIRITS
PRESENTS:

# BLADE
CALIFORNIA STYLE
# GIN

Davorin Kuchan, Master Distiller

12% FINE GRAPE SPIRITS
88% VODKA
47% ALC.BY VOL

PRODUCED AND BOTTLED BY
OLD WORLD SPIRITS, LLC
BELMONT, CALIFORNIA
USA

**750 ML**
WWW.BLADEGIN.COM

GOVERNMENT WARNING:(1) ACCORDING TO THE SURGEON GENERAL, WOMEN SHOULD NOT DRINK ALCOHOLIC BEVERAGES DURING PREGNANCY BECAUSE OF THE RISK OF BIRTH DEFECTS. (2) CONSUMPTION OF ALCOHOLIC BEVERAGES IMPAIRS YOUR ABILITY TO DRIVE A CAR OR OPERATE MACHINERY, AND MAY CAUSE HEALTH PROBLEMS.

7 98304 09451 0

---

Type: Barrel Aged Gin
Production: Single Barrel
Date Distilled: Sept 17, 2009
Date Barreled: Sept 22, 2009
Formula: BG 5-09
Base Spirit: Wheat GNS, Zinfandel Eau De Vie 2x distilled
Dist. Proof: 737 Hearts Run
Barrel Type: French Limousin Oak 4T / TH Previously Zin
Filtration: Plate Filter Sterile 0.5 u
Age: 13 Months
Bottle Proof: 124 / 62% ABV

Distiller's Notes:
Ageing Blade Gin rounded out brite citrus and cilantro notes. Zinfandel Eau De Vie matured gracefully into rich Allambic brandy - floral tones complement vanilla and caramel born from the toasted French Limousin Oak. Juniper and black cardamom released bright pine spice with rich, holiday flair.

Davorin Kuchan, Master Distiller

**LIMITED EDITION**
**- CASK STRENGTH -**
**SINGLE BARREL AGED GIN**
**AGED 15 MONTHS**

**K&L SINGLE BARREL SERIES**

88% GRAIN NEUTRAL SPIRITS
12% FINE GRAPE SPIRITS
62% ALC.BY VOL

DISTILLED & BOTTLED BY

OLD WORLD SPIRITS

BELMONT CALIFORNIA USA

**750 ML**

GOVERNMENT WARNING:(1) ACCORDING TO THE SURGEON GENERAL, WOMEN SHOULD NOT DRINK ALCOHOLIC BEVERAGES DURING PREGNANCY BECAUSE OF THE RISK OF BIRTH DEFECTS. (2) CONSUMPTION OF ALCOHOLIC BEVERAGES IMPAIRS YOUR ABILITY TO DRIVE A CAR OR OPERATE MACHINERY, AND MAY CAUSE HEALTH PROBLEMS.

7 98304 14460 4

handmade in
small batches

Distilled & Bottled by Peach Street Distillers
Palisade, Colorado
750 ml  ALC/VOL 40% (80 PROOF)

## Label 1 (left)

⑫ 45% ALC/VOL
(90 PROOF)

PINK SPRUCE

**ROGUE**
*Spirits*

**GIN** 750 ML

Seasoned in Oregon
Pinot Barrels

## Label 2 (center-left)

HONORING UNIQUE
ROGUES WHOSE SPIRIT
LINGERS LONG PAST THEIR
MORTAL EXISTENCE.

In the 1800s Oregon loggers
used handsaws and oxen to
harvest timber.  The lumber
was used to build ships and
homes across the country and
was traded as far away as
China and Japan.

12 Ingredients: spruce oil,
cucumber, juniper berries,
angelica root, orange peel,
lemon peel, coriander,
ginger, orris root, grains of
paradise, tangerine oil,
free range coastal water.

DISTILLED FROM GRAIN

www.rogue.com

DISTILLED & BOTTLED BY
ROGUE ALES
NEWPORT, OR  97365 U.S.A.

GOVERNMENT WARNING:
(1) ACCORDING TO THE SURGEON
GENERAL, WOMEN SHOULD NOT DRINK
ALCOHOLIC BEVERAGES DURING
PREGNANCY BECAUSE OF THE RISK OF
BIRTH DEFECTS. (2) CONSUMPTION OF
ALCOHOLIC BEVERAGES IMPAIRS YOUR
ABILITY TO DRIVE A CAR OR OPERATE
MACHINERY, AND MAY CAUSE  HEALTH
PROBLEMS.

0  95301  14408  9

## Label 3 (center-right)

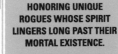

HONORING UNIQUE
ROGUES WHOSE SPIRIT
LINGERS LONG PAST THEIR
MORTAL EXISTENCE.

In the 1800s Oregon loggers
used handsaws and oxen to
harvest timber.  The lumber
was used to build ships and
homes across the country and
was traded as far away as
China and Japan.

12 Ingredients: spruce oil,
cucumber, juniper berries,
angelica root, orange peel,
lemon peel, coriander,
ginger, orris root, grains of
paradise, tangerine,
free range coastal water.

www.rogue.com

DISTILLED & BOTTLED BY
ROGUE ALES
NEWPORT, OR  97365  U.S.A.

GOVERNMENT WARNING:
(1) ACCORDING TO THE SURGEON
GENERAL, WOMEN SHOULD NOT DRINK
ALCOHOLIC BEVERAGES DURING
PREGNANCY BECAUSE OF THE RISK OF
BIRTH DEFECTS. (2) CONSUMPTION OF
ALCOHOLIC BEVERAGES IMPAIRS YOUR
ABILITY TO DRIVE A CAR OR OPERATE
MACHINERY, AND MAY CAUSE  HEALTH
PROBLEMS.

0  95301  14404  1

## Label 4 (right)

Circa 1885

⑫ 45% ALC/VOL
(90 PROOF)

SPRUCE

**ROGUE**
*Spirits*

**GIN** 750 ML

ARTISAN
DISTILLED IN
OREGON

# COMB 9
## GIN

*New York Dry Gin*

### 750 ML
47% ALCOHOL BY VOL • 94 PROOF

## Taste the craft of COMB 9.

COMB 9 is our contribution to the resurgence of gin in cocktails. We start with the honey spirit used in our vodka, and gently distill it with juniper, lavender, rose, citrus peel, galangal and other selected botanicals to give COMB 9 a unique floral nose and a refined finish.

Why do we call it COMB 9? Well, it could be that it took 9 different recipes until we were satisfied, or for our 9 botanicals or maybe because we scribbled a 9 on the 9th proof of our label and it was printed by mistake. Whichever it is, try COMB 9 in a martini, in a favorite cocktail or experiment with something new. Taste the difference of our quality artisan spirits.

*Distiller/Proprietor*

DISTILLED FROM HONEY

DISTILLED AND BOTTLED BY
**STILLTHEONE DISTILLERY LLC**
PORT CHESTER, NY

**GOVERNMENT WARNING:** (1) According to the Surgeon General, women should not drink alcoholic beverages during pregnancy because of the risk of birth defects. (2) Consumption of alcoholic beverages impairs your ability to drive a car or operate machinery and may cause health problems.

750 ML ● 47% ALCOHOL BY VOL ● 94 PROOF

8 53591 00201 0

An American style Gin using eight botanicals is well balanced using Juniper & hops to create this unique spirit.

Cheers! visit us at www.SquareOneBrewery.com!

8  50038 00302  9

ARTISAN SPIRITS          ARTISAN SPIRITS

Small Batch Handcrafted          Made in the United States

Spirits of St. Louis

# REGATTA BAY
## GIN
100% GRAIN NEUTRAL SPIRITS

Spirits of St. Louis
40% ALC./VOL. (80 PROOF)

750ml

DISTILLED AND BOTTLED BY SQUARE ONE BREWERY AND DISTILLERY - ST. LOUIS, MO.

GOVERNMENT WARNING: (1) ACCORDING TO THE SURGEON GENERAL WOMEN SHOULD NOT DRINK ALCOHOLIC BEVERAGES DURING PREGNANCY BECAUSE OF THE RISK OF BIRTH DEFECTS. (2) CONSUMPTION OF ALCOHOLIC BEVERAGES IMPAIRS YOUR ABILITY TO DRIVE A CAR OR OPERATE MACHINERY AND MAY CAUSE HEALTH PROBLEMS.

**DISTILLED & BOTTLED BY
PACIFIC DISTILLERY LLC
WOODINVILLE, WA USA**

www.pacificdistillery.com

**GOVERNMENT WARNING:** (1) ACCORDING TO THE SURGEON GENERAL WOMEN SHOULD NOT DRINK ALCOHOLIC BEVERAGES DURING PREGNANCY BECAUSE OF THE RISK OF BIRTH DEFECTS. (2) CONSUMPTION OF ALCOHOLIC BEVERAGES IMPAIRS YOUR ABILITY TO DRIVE A CAR OR OPERATE MACHINERY, AND MAY CAUSE HEALTH PROBLEMS.

898322 00206 8

# VOYAGER

EXTRA-FINE    SMALL-BATCH

## DISTILLED

### Dry Gin

*Distilled in copper alembics
from select choice botanicals.*

750 ML          42% ALC/VOL (84 PROOF)

Voyager Dry Gin is created using only the finest hand-selected whole botanicals from around the world, using only 19th century artisan distiller techniques.

Our gin is distilled in small batches, by hand, in an authentic copper alembic potstill ensuring Old World artistry and craftsmanship.

Voyager is crafted with the following traditional botanicals:

- JUNIPER
- CORIANDER
- LICORICE ROOT
- CARDAMOM
- ANISEED
- LEMON
- ORANGE
- ORRIS
- ANGELICA
- CASSIA

Distilled from 100%
Grain Neutral Spirits

# GRAPPA

Traditional grappa made from locally
grown Gewurztraminer grapes

*Grappa*

Distilled and bottled by Peach Street
Distillers, Palisade Colorado with
the beloved assistance of
Debeque Canyon Winery

375 ml ALC/VOL 40% (80 PROOF)

ESSENTIAL SPIRITS · ALAMBIC DISTILLERIES

CLASSICK
GRAPPA

RICH AROMAS WITH
ORIGINAL GRAPE FLAVOR

*Grape*
*Cabernet Sauvignon*
*Grown in*
*Stag's Leap District*
*Napa California 2004*

375ml

40% ALC. BY VOL. (80 PROOF)

GREAT LAKES
DISTILLERY
*Artisan Series*

GRAPPA

*A Product of Wisconsin*

40% ALC By Volume

GOVERNMENT WARNING: (1) ACCORDING TO THE SURGEON GENERAL, WOMEN SHOULD NOT DRINK ALCOHOLIC BEVERAGES DURING PREGNANCY BECAUSE OF THE RISK OF BIRTH DEFECTS. (2) CONSUMPTIONS OF ALCOHOLIC BEVERAGES IMPAIRS YOUR ABILITY TO DRIVE A CAR OR OPERATE MACHINERY AND MAY CAUSE HEALTH PROBLEMS.

FIORE

GRAPPA

Alcohol By Volume 40%
375 ml

**Produced and bottled by Fiore Winery Inc.;Pylesville, MD 21132**
www.fiorewinery.com
(410) 879-4007      Contains Sulfates      BW-MD-38

# CLEAR CREEK DISTILLERY

Fresh Oregon muscat grape pomace distilled into powerful, fragrant, classic grappa.

OREGON MUSCAT

Grappa

fermented, distilled, and bottled by
Clear Creek Distillery      Portland, Oregon USA.

375ml.      alcohol 40% by vol.      (80 proof)

# LIQUEUR

CLEAR CREEK DISTILLERY

*Oregon Cranberry Liqueur*

ALCOHOL 19.56% BY VOLUME (39.12 PROOF)

McMENAMINS
**EDGEFIELD**
DISTILLERY

COFFEE LIQUEUR
750ml • ALCOHOL 20% BY VOLUME • 40 PROOF

**HOLZ'S**
APPLE CRISP
—LIQUEUR—

1 LTR. • 15% ALC.
CONTAINS NO ARTIFICIAL FLAVORS OR COLORS
REFRIGERATE AFTER OPENING

PRODUCED BY: YAHARA BAY DISTILLERS

ST. GE

## AMERICAN FRUITS

### BLACK CURRANT CORDIAL

PRODUCED & BOTTLED BY
WARWICK VALLEY WINE CO. INC.,
WARWICK, NEW YORK, 10990

www.wvwinery.com

375 ml.          18% alc/vol

## AMERICAN FRUITS

BOURBON BARREL AGED 12 MONTHS
### APPLE LIQUEUR

PRODUCED & BOTTLED BY
WARWICK VALLEY WINE CO. INC.,
WARWICK, NEW YORK, 10990

www.wvwinery.com

375 ml.          19.5% alc/vol

M·A·U·I
'Ōkolehao Liqueur

ALC. 40% BY VOL.

DISTILLED AND BOTTLED ON MAUI BY
HALEAKALA DISTILLERS
MAKAWAO, MAUI, HI USA

www.mauirum.biz

750 ML.

GOVERNMENT WARNING: (1) ACCORDING TO THE SURGEON GENERAL, WOMEN SHOULD NOT DRINK ALCOHOLIC BEVERAGES DURING PREGNANCY BECAUSE OF THE RISK OF BIRTH DEFECTS. (2) CONSUMPTION OF ALCOHOLIC BEVERAGES IMPAIRS YOUR ABILITY TO DRIVE A CAR OR OPERATE MACHINERY, AND MAY CAUSE HEALTH PROBLEMS.

# STRINGER'S ORCHARD

*Plum Liqueur*

## PACIFIC PLUM

*Produced from the wild and rare native Pacific Plum found growing in a relatively limited region of southern Oregon and northern California.*

40% alc. by vol.
(80 Proof)

www.StringersOrchard.com

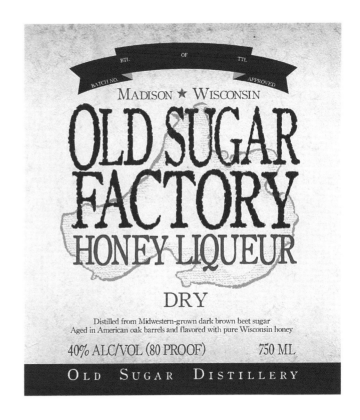

MADISON ★ WISCONSIN

# OLD SUGAR FACTORY
## HONEY LIQUEUR

### DRY

Distilled from Midwestern-grown dark brown beet sugar
Aged in American oak barrels and flavored with pure Wisconsin honey

40% ALC/VOL (80 PROOF)          750 ML

OLD SUGAR DISTILLERY

**GINGER
HONEY**

PINEAPPLE
JALAPEÑO

PINEAPPLE
JALAPEÑO
FLAVORED LIQUEUR

PRODUCED & BOTTLED
BY
TRIPLE EIGHT
DISTILLERY
NANTUCKET, MA

30% alc/vol (60 proof)
750ml

TRIPLE EIGHT

DISTILLERY
nantucket island

GOVERNMENT WARNING: (1) ACCORDING TO THE SURGEON GENERAL, WOMEN SHOULD NOT DRINK ALCOHOLIC BEVERAGES DURING PREGNANCY BECAUSE OF THE RISK OF BIRTH DEFECTS. (2) CONSUMPTION OF ALCOHOLIC BEVERAGES IMPAIRS YOUR ABILITY TO DRIVE A CAR OR OPERATE MACHINERY, AND MAY CAUSE HEALTH PROBLEMS.

**GINGER
HONEY**
FLAVORED LIQUEUR

PRODUCED & BOTTLED
BY
TRIPLE EIGHT
DISTILLERY
NANTUCKET, MA

30% alc/vol (60 proof)
750ml

HUIXOC
COFFEE

TRIPLE EIGHT

DISTILLERY
nantucket island

HUIXOC
COFFEE
FLAVORED LIQUEUR

PRODUCED & BOTTLED
BY
TRIPLE EIGHT
DISTILLERY
NANTUCKET, MA

# MOONSHINE

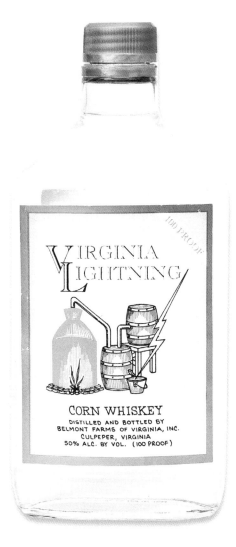

FLAGLER
LIGHTNING
*Spirit Conjurors & Alchemists*

Florida
CORN
WHISKY
Flagler Spirits
Aged Less Than 30 Days

HAND CRAFTED IN
SMALL BATCHES

BATCH 10D16A

50 % ALC./VOL. (100° PROOF) 750ML

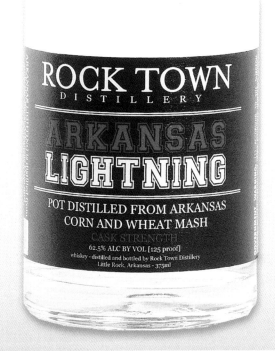

ROCK TOWN
D I S T I L L E R Y

ARKANSAS
LIGHTNING

POT DISTILLED FROM ARKANSAS
CORN AND WHEAT MASH

CASK STRENGTH

62.5% ALC BY VOL [125 proof]
whiskey - distilled and bottled by Rock Town Distillery
Little Rock, Arkansas - 375ml

KINGS COUNTY DISTILLERY
moonshine
corn whiskey 200ml
40% alcohol by volume

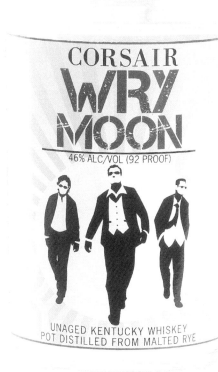

CORSAIR
WRY
MOON
46% ALC/VOL (92 PROOF)

UNAGED KENTUCKY WHISKEY
POT DISTILLED FROM MALTED RYE

WOODINVILLE
*handcrafted organic spirits*
WHISKEY CO.

HEADLONG

WHITE DOG
WHISKEY

40% ALC/VOL

Made in
 hington State

# RUM

40% ALC/VOL     750ML

# COPPER RUN

★ ★ ★

AMERICAN
GOLD RUM

DISTILLED AND BOTTLED BY
COPPER RUN DISTILLERY

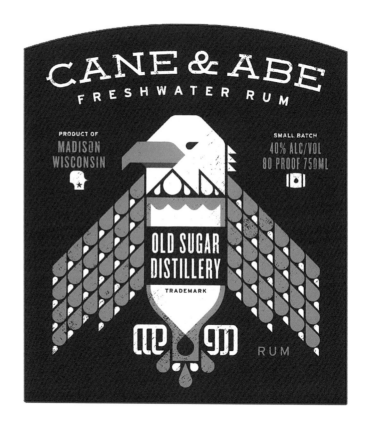

CANE & ABE
FRESHWATER RUM

PRODUCT OF
MADISON
WISCONSIN

SMALL BATCH
40% ALC/VOL
80 PROOF 750ML

OLD SUGAR
DISTILLERY

TRADEMARK

RUM

Sergeant
**Classick**™

SILVER
**RUM**

POT DISTILLED
FROM 100%
HAWAIIAN MOLASSES

750 ml        ALC 40% by VOL (80 proof)

*The Spirit of Hawaii*®

Sergeant
**Classick**™

GOLD
**RUM**

POT DISTILLED
FROM 100%
HAWAIIAN MOLASSES

750 ml        ALC 40% by VOL (80 proof)

The Spirit
of Hawaii®

'Sgt.' Dave Classick, a highly decorated Vietnam veteran, returned from combat and fell in love with the Hawaiian Islands. In seeking his true vocation, he discovered a talent for making (as well as drinking) fine rum. And thus, seeing the islands with sugar cane stretching as far as the eye could see, he set out to create his own.

*The Old Sugar Mill*

Now you too can share in Sgt. Classick's affection for exotic spirits. Crafted in the traditional manner of fine rum makers the world over: each batch is hand-distilled in the finest alambic copper pot stills and gathered in pails a few drops at a time. Sgt. Classick's rum has a depth of flavor unlike any rum you've ever tasted.

COLORADO

Montanya
RUM

Oro

AWARD WINNING + OBSESSIVELY CRAFTED

HIGH MOUNTAIN RUM

40% ALC./VOL. (80 PROOF) 750 ML

COLORADO

Montanya
RUM

platino

AWARD WINNING + OBSESSIVELY CRAFTED

HIGH MOUNTAIN RUM

40% ALC/VOL (80 PROOF) 750 ML

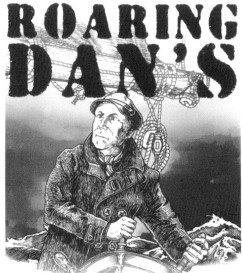

ROARING
DAN'S

MAPLE FLAVORED RUM

750ml. 45% Alcohol by Vol. 90 Proof

80 PROOF

Fine Rum

PRICHARD'S

F I N E    R U M

BOTTLED AT BARREL PROOF

DISTILLED AND BOTTLED EXCLUSIVELY BY
PRICHARDS DISTILLERY, INC
KELSO, TENNESSEE

40% ALC/VOL    750 ML

MAD ☆ BIRD
-Y-    -B-
RUM
750ML    40% ALC/VOL
HAND-CRAFT DISTILLED IN MADISON, WI

Dogfish Head
Wit Spiced Rhum

A sublime & distinct
thrice-distilled,
handcrafted white rum
with curacao, orange peel
& coriander.

40% Alc. by Vol.    750 ML

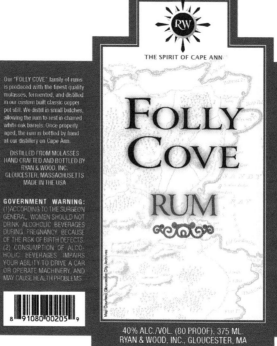

THE SPIRIT OF CAPE ANN

Our "FOLLY COVE" family of rums is produced with the finest quality molasses, fermented, and distilled in our custom built classic copper pot still. We distill in small batches, allowing the rum to rest in charred white oak barrels. Once properly aged, the rum is bottled by hand at our distillery on Cape Ann.

DISTILLED FROM MOLASSES HAND CRAFTED AND BOTTLED BY RYAN & WOOD, INC. GLOUCESTER, MASSACHUSETTS MADE IN THE USA

GOVERNMENT WARNING: (1) ACCORDING TO THE SURGEON GENERAL, WOMEN SHOULD NOT DRINK ALCOHOLIC BEVERAGES DURING PREGNANCY, BECAUSE OF THE RISK OF BIRTH DEFECTS. (2) CONSUMPTION OF ALCO-HOLIC BEVERAGES IMPAIRS YOUR ABILITY TO DRIVE A CAR OR OPERATE MACHINERY, AND MAY CAUSE HEALTH PROBLEMS.

8 91080 00205 9

# FOLLY COVE

## RUM

40% ALC./VOL. (80 PROOF), 375 ML.
RYAN & WOOD, INC., GLOUCESTER, MA

FOLLY COVE, rich in Gloucester's history, is famous for its many shipwrecks. Smugglers of all types came into this cove seeking safety, only to find they were dangerously off course.

Now known for scuba divers searching for the shipwrecks and lobstermen plying their trade, Folly Cove is one of the most beautiful areas of Cape Ann's coastline.

For more information about Ryan & Wood, Inc., Distilleries, and the fascinating history of FOLLY COVE go to: www.ryanandwood.com

THE SPIRIT OF CAPE ANN

DIELINE
WILL NOT PRINT

VARNISH-FREE AREA

Edward Teach ~ Black Beard
1679/81 - 1718

40% ALC/VOL
80 PROOF

# ROGUE
## Spirits

## DARK RUM

750 ML

ARTISAN
DISTILLED IN
OREGON

HONORING UNIQUE
ROGUES WHOSE SPIRIT
LINGERS LONG PAST THEIR
MORTAL EXISTENCE.

The sight of Blackbeard was enough to make victims surrender without a fight. At 6' 5", he would weave wicks laced with gunpowder in his beard and light them during battle. If his victims surrendered without a fight, he would take the goods, weapons, and rum and allow them to sail away. If he met resistance, he would maroon the crew and burn the ship.

"Only the devil and I know the whereabouts of my treasure, and the one of us who lives the longest should take it all."

## DOUBLE DISTILLED
## & BOTTLED BY ROGUE ALES
## PORTLAND, OR 97209 U.S.A

GOVERNMENT WARNING:
(1) ACCORDING TO THE SURGEON GENERAL, WOMEN SHOULD NOT DRINK ALCOHOLIC BEVERAGES DURING PREGNANCY BECAUSE OF THE RISK OF BIRTH DEFECTS. (2) CONSUMPTION OF ALCOHOLIC BEVERAGES IMPAIRS YOUR ABILITY TO DRIVE A CAR OR OPERATE MACHINERY, AND MAY CAUSE HEALTH PROBLEMS.

0  95301 14402  7

**RAILEAN**

**TEXAS**
*Gulf Coast Rum*

**Small Cask Reserve**
*Single-Barrel*

40% Alc./Vol.                    750 ml.

HANDCRAFTED

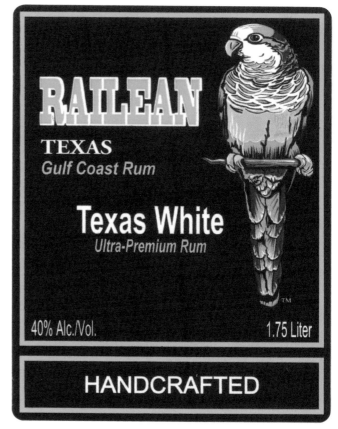

**RAILEAN**

**TEXAS**
*Gulf Coast Rum*

**Texas White**
*Ultra-Premium Rum*

40% Alc./Vol.                    1.75 Liter

HANDCRAFTED

ARTISAN SPIRITS         ARTISAN SPIRITS

*Small Batch Handcrafted*     *Made in the United States*

# ISLAND TIME
## AMBER
## RUM

## Spirits of St. Louis
### 40% ALC./VOL. (80 PROOF)

DISTILLED AND BOTTLED BY SQUARE ONE BREWERY AND DISTILLERY - ST. LOUIS, MO.

Our hand crafted Rum is made with only the finest ingredients, including Golden Cane Molasses from the sugar fields of Louisiana & fine sweet water in the United States from right here in St. Louis. Like all of our Rums, one sip will take you back to your favorite Island. Two sips and your back on vacation. So relax & enjoy - you're on Island Time!

Cheers! visit us at www.SquareOneBrewery.com!

**GOVERNMENT WARNING:** (1) ACCORDING TO THE SURGEON GENERAL, WOMEN SHOULD NOT DRINK ALCOHOLIC BEVERAGES DURING PREGNANCY BECAUSE OF THE RISK OF BIRTH DEFECTS. (2) CONSUMPTION OF ALCOHOLIC BEVERAGES IMPAIRS YOUR ABILITY TO DRIVE A CAR OR OPERATE MACHINERY AND MAY CAUSE HEALTH PROBLEMS.

750ml

8 50038 00300 5

# VODKA

ESTABLISHED 1996
B
BENDISTILLERY

# CRATER LAKE

## Hand Crafted American

## Vodka

100% Natural Grain Spirits

Filtered 10 times through charcoal & crushed lava

750 ML

80 PROOF ALCOHOL   40% BY VOLUME

BARDENAY

*Premium Recipe*

# VODKA

DISTILLED

*from*

CANE SUGAR

DISTILLED AND BOTTLED BY
BARDENAY, INC., COEUR D'ALENE, IDAHO

NET CONTENTS          40% ALC/VOL
750 ML                80 PROOF

# SPIRIT
## OF THE HUDSON
# VODKA

**Triple-Distilled In
The Hudson Valley**

375 ml ~ 40% alc/vol

Artisan Distilled From 100% NY Apples
And Bottled By:
Tuthilltown Spirits, Gardiner, NY
www.tuthilltown.com

# CHASE™
★ MADE IN ★
# NEBRASKA
# VODKA

EST. 2009

**HANDCRAFTED
IN SMALL BATCHES**

— DISTILLED FROM GRAIN —

**COOPER'S CHASE DISTILLERY
WEST POINT, NE**

40%ALC/VOL (80 PROOF)  750ML

IT WILL LEAVE AN INDELIBLE
MARK ON YOUR SOUL.

# Ink

## VODKA
Distilled from
Washington State Grain
40 % Alc by Vol (80 proof)

# OYO
## VODKa

A smooth, small-batch,
artisanal vodka made of Ohio's
soft, red winter wheat.

40% Alc. by Vol.       1 unit: 750 Ml
(80 Proof)            Batch #

*DISTILLED IN COLUMBUS OHIO, US*

GRAIN ~ TO ~ GLASS

[blood + sweat + tears of joy]

HAND CRAFTED ON CAPITOL HILL · SEATTLE, WA · OOLA IND.

# /VODKA/

| BATCH NO. | CASE NO. | MASTER DISTILLER: |
|---|---|---|
| 3 | 1 | |
| ALCOHOL/VOL. 45 % | PROOF 90 | VOL. 750 ML |

MIDWEST

*American*
VODKA

DISTILLED FROM GRAINS

*From the Heartland*

40% ALC. BY VOL.                    ONE LITER

*Tito's*®

AWARD WINNING
DISTILLED 6 TIMES

*Handmade*

VODKA

Crafted in an Old Fashioned Pot Still
by America's Original Microdistillery

AUSTIN ★ TEXAS

DISTILLED & BOTTLED BY FIFTH GENERATION, INC. AUSTIN, TX. 40% ALC./VOL.

# PLANTATION™

## Handcrafted

**Thirteenth Colony Distilleries**
**Georgia's only small batch distillery**
40% alc./vol. (80 proof)  750 ml

# VODKA

*Quail in Flight* by David Lanier, 2008 Georgia Artist of the year, is proudly featured on the Plantation Vodka label. Posters, reproductions and original artwork by David Lanier are available at **www.plantationgallery.com** or visit Plantation Gallery, Inc., 2607 Stuart Avenue, Albany, Georgia 31707 (229) 883 0111.

500  DING TO
SHOULD
DURING
F BIRTH
DEFECTS. (2) CONSUMPTION OF ALCOHOLIC BEVERAGES IMPAIRS YOUR ABILITY TO DRIVE A CAR OR OPERATE MACHINERY, AND MAY CAUSE HEALTH PROBLEMS.

7  66139 30000  7

PLANTATION VODKA is the result of Dr. Gil Klemann's quest to make the ultimate vodka. PLANTATION VODKA is handcrafted in small batches and carbon filtered for smoothness by Georgia's only craft distillery which is located in the heart of Plantation Country. Handcrafted by friends for friends... simply the best! Please drink responsibly. Visit **www.plantationvodka.com** for more information.

**Distilled from Grain**
**made by Thirteenth Colony**
**Distilleries, LLC**
**Americus, Georgia**

*SLOOP*
**BETTY**™

HAND-CRAFTED
WHEAT VODKA

Alc. 40% by Vol. (80 PROOF)    750 ml

HANGAR ONE VODKA

VODKA
"straight"

VODKA
PRODUCED AND BOTTLED BY ST GEORGE SPIRITS
ALAMEDA, CALIFORNIA

750 ML 40% ALC /VOL.

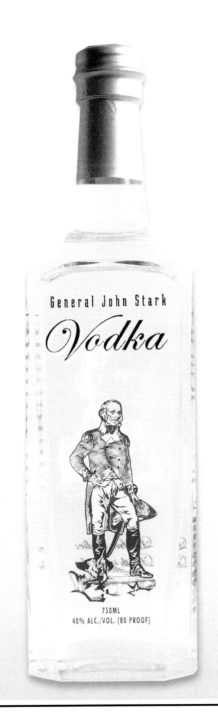

CORE

VODKA

SMALL BATCH DISTILLED
*from*
HUDSON VALLEY APPLES

40% ALC/VOL
375 ML

Batch No. 12  Bottle No. 174

KOENIG
DISTILLERY

FAMOUS
IDAHO® POTATO
VODKA

40% ALC/VOL (80 PROOF) 750 ml

# NEW DEAL
# VODKA

40% ALC/VOL

LOCALLY FLAVORED VODKA
DISTILLED & BOTTLED BY
NEW DEAL DISTILLERY LLC
PORTLAND, OREGON

44% ALC/VOL (88 PROOF)
DISTILLED & BOTTLED BY NEW DEAL DISTILLERY LLC PORTLAND, OREGON

# INFUSED VODKA

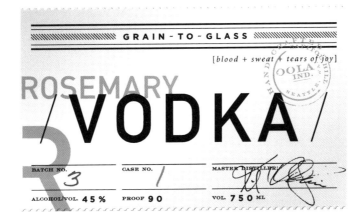

# HUCKLEBERRY

MADE WITH
IDAHO
WILD HUCKLEBERRIES

## KOENIG
### DISTILLERY

Ⓚ

## HUCKLEBERRY
## FLAVORED VODKA

35% ALC/VOL (70 PROOF) 750 ml

# OYO
## Honey
## Vanilla Bean

A smooth, small-batch, flavored vodka
made of Ohio's soft, red winter wheat.

40% Alc. by Vol.
(80 Proof)

1 unit: 750 Ml

DISTILLED IN
COLUMBUS
OHIO, US

Honey Vanilla
Flavored Vodka

Batch #

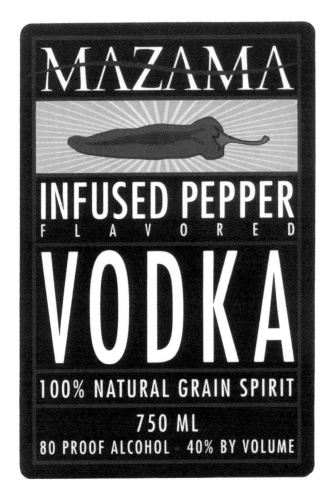

# WHISKEY

152 SANTA FE SPIRITS

152 BERKSHIRE MOUNTAIN
DISTILLERS

153 AMERICAN CRAFT
WHISKEY DISTILLERY

153 THIRTEENTH COLONY
DISTILLERIES

154 ERNEST SCARANO
DISTILLERY

155 ERNEST SCARANO
DISTILLERY

155 WYLIE HOWELL SPIRITS

156 BALLAST POINT SPIRITS

156 BAINBRIDGE
ORGANIC DISTILLERS

157 BALCONES DISTILLING

158 WOODSTONE CREEK
DISTILLERY

158 ANCHOR BREWING
& DISTILLING

159 DRYFLY DISTILLING

160 COPPER FOX

161 BALCONES DISTILLING

162 FINGER LAKES DISTILLING

162 CORSAIR ARTISAN DISTILLERS

163 MCMENAMINS EDGEFIELD
DISTILLERY

163 KOVAL DISTILLERY

164 NEW HOLLAND ARTISAN SPIRITS

164 ROGUE HOUSE OF SPIRITS

165 TUTHILLTOWN SPIRITS

165 LYONS SPIRITS

166 FINGER LAKES DISTILLING

166 BRECKENRIDGE BREWERY

167 GARRISON BROS. DISTILLERY

167 COPPER FOX

168 COPPER RUN DISTILLERY

168 NEW HOLLAND SPIRITS

169 DANCING PINES DISTILLERY

169 CATOCTIN CREEK DISTILLERY

170 STONE BARN BRANDY WORKS

170 HIGH WEST DISTILLERY

171 LOUISVILLE DISTILLERY

172 HIGH WEST DISTILLERY

173 DOWNSLOPE DISTILLING

173 ST. JAMES SPIRITS

174 MCMENAMINS EDGEFIELD
DISTILLERY

174 NASHOBA VALLEY SPIRITS

175 REBECCA CREEK DISTILLERY

176 KOVAL DISTILLERY

177 STRANAHAN'S COLORADO
WHISKEY

178 CEDAR RIDGE DISTILLERY

178 ISAIAH MORGAN DISTILLERY

179 JOURNEYMAN DISTILLERY

179 PINCHGUT HOLLOW
DISTILLERY

180 OOLA DISTILLERY

180 STILLWATER SPIRITS

181 SQUARE ONE DISTILLERY

181 MOUNTAIN LAUREL SPIRITS

182 PRICHARD'S DISTILLERY

182 ROUGHSTOCK

183 HIGH PLAINS DISTILLERY

183 TEMPLETON RYE

184 WOODINVILLE WHISKEY CO.

185 TUTHILLTOWN SPIRITS

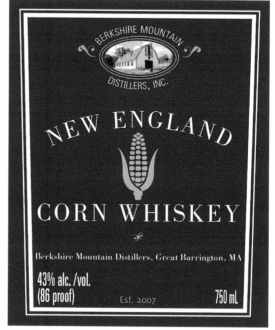

AMERICAN CRAFT WHISKEY DISTILLERY

# LOW GAP
WHISKEY

CLEAR

DISTILLED FROM MALTED BAVARIAN HARD WHEAT

CRAFT-METHOD
HAND DISTILLATION

ANTIQUE DOUBLE-DISTILLATION
COPPER POTSTILL

........................................................................................

BATCH № 2010/3B   44.8% alcohol by volume

distilled April 19, 2010   aged 357 minutes in oak

845   750 ML bottles filled July 27, 2010

LIMITED RELEASE

13th Colony
southern
corn whiskey

Bottle/Batch №
Approved by

750 ml   47.5 AlC/VOL   (95 Proof)

# "HAY FEVER"

SIPPING WHISKEY MADE FRO!
THE 3RD CUTTING OF HAY
HICKMAN FARMS, ELMORE OHIO

BOTTLED BY
ERNEST SCARANO DISTILLERY
GIBSONBURG, OHIO 43431

2010

70% A.B.V.              140 PROOF

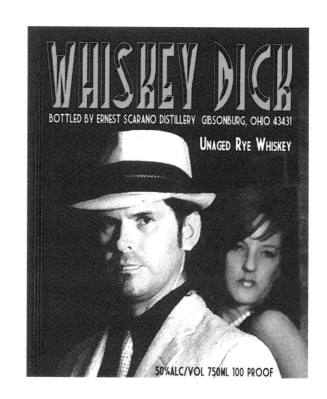

BALCONES
BABY BLUE
made with 100% blue corn.

750 ml.     CORN WHISKY     46% ALC/VOL

TEXAS MADE     ★     HANDCRAFTED

BALCONES
RUMBLE
A TEXAS WILDFLOWER HONEY, TURBINADO SUGAR AND MISSION FIG SPIRIT

750 ml.     47% Alc. by Vol.     Distilled Spirits Specialty

batch number: R10-10     bottling date: 5-20-10     distiller: CT

SILVER MEDAL
2010

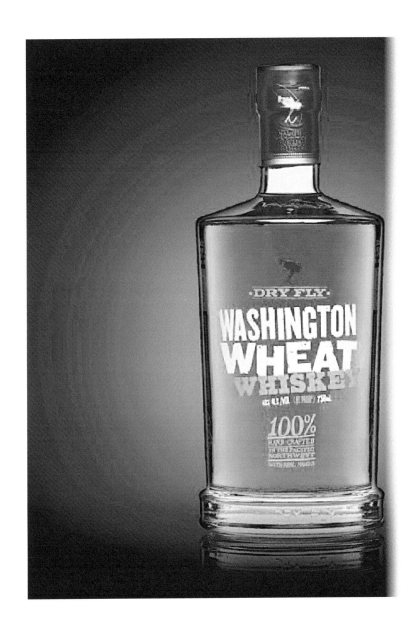

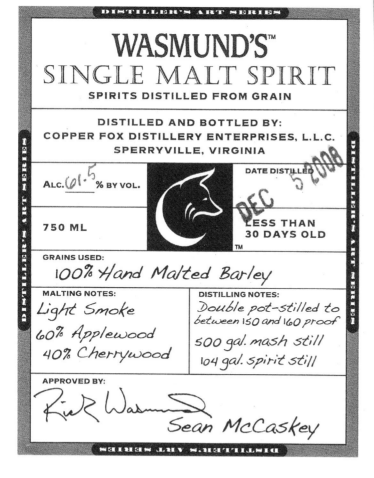

**DISTILLER'S ART SERIES**

# WASMUND'S™
## SINGLE MALT SPIRIT
**SPIRITS DISTILLED FROM GRAIN**

**DISTILLED AND BOTTLED BY:**
**COPPER FOX DISTILLERY ENTERPRISES, L.L.C.**
**SPERRYVILLE, VIRGINIA**

ALC. 61.5 % BY VOL.

DATE DISTILLED

DEC 5 2008

750 ML

**LESS THAN 30 DAYS OLD**

**GRAINS USED:**
100% Hand Malted Barley

**MALTING NOTES:**
Light Smoke
60% Applewood
40% Cherrywood

**DISTILLING NOTES:**
Double pot-stilled to between 150 and 160 proof
500 gal. mash still
104 gal. spirit still

**APPROVED BY:**
Rick Wasmund
Sean McCaskey

**DISTILLER'S ART SERIES**

# WASMUND'S
**RAPPAHANNOCK**
*pot stilled*
NON CHILL-FILTERED
## SINGLE MALT WHISKY
*Naturally flavored and colored with toasted Applewood, Cherrywood and Oak*

DISTILLED AND BOTTLED BY COPPER FOX
DISTILLERY ENTERPRISES, L.L.C.
SPERRYVILLE, VIRGINIA

750 ML
48% ALC. BY VOLUME (96 PROOF)          Batch No. _____

# BALCONES
## BRIMSTONE
made with 100% blue corn.

### TEXAS SCRUB OAK SMOKED
## CORN WHISKY

750 ml.                    53% Alc/Vol

# EDGEFIELD DISTILLERY

## HOGSHEAD

### Whiskey

**Pure Pot Distilled
from
100% Malted Barley**

**750 ML
ALCOHOL 46%
BY VOLUME (92 PROOF)**

# KOVAL

*ORGANIC*

## RYE CHICAGO
### WHISKEY
DISTILLED FROM 100% RYE

Ⓤ

USDA ORGANIC

40% ALC BY VOL          750mL

HUDSON
NEW YORK CORN
WHISKEY

750 ml    46% alc/vol

Pot Distilled From 100% New York Corn

Hand Crafted and Bottled By:
Tuthilltown Spirits, Gardiner, New York

PEARSE LYONS
RESERVE™

WHISKEY

40% ALC/VOL

80 PROOF

750ml

BOURBON WHISKEY
an american classic - a local legend

Small Batched Bourbon Whiskey
Barrel Aged Less Than 4 Years
44% Alc by Vol - 88 Proof   750 ML

DANCING
PINES
DISTILLERY

CATOCTIN
CREEK™

*ORGANIC*
Roundstone Rye
WHISKY
DISTILLED FROM 100% RYE

NATURALLY DISTILLED AND BOTTLED
IN LOUDOUN COUNTY VIRGINIA
FROM HIGHEST QUALITY INGREDIENTS

CATOCTIN CREEK DISTILLING COMPANY, LLC
PURCELLVILLE, VIRGINIA

ALYSON ½ PETER

40% ALC. BY VOL.                    750 mL

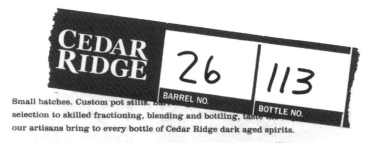

# CEDAR RIDGE

**26** | **113**

BARREL NO. | BOTTLE NO.

Small batches. Custom pot stills. Ba...
selection to skilled fractioning, blending and bottling, taste...
our artisans bring to every bottle of Cedar Ridge dark aged spirits.

**750** ML   **40%** ALC BY VOL.

## IOWA BOURBON
# WHISKEY

For the best in bourbon, go straight to the heart of corn country. Cedar Ridge
Bourbon is built on a base of corn whiskey, barley and rye. Artisans guide the
nation's favorite blend through distillation, charcoal filtering and aging. This
is the best of the Midwest in a bottle. Enjoy!   MASTER DISTILLER

750 ML   40% ALC BY VOL.

GOVERNMENT WARNING: (1) ACCORDING TO THE SURGEON GENERAL, WOMEN SHOULD NOT DRINK ALCOHOLIC BEVERAGES DURING PREGNANCY BECAUSE OF THE RISK OF BIRTH DEFECTS. (2) CONSUMPTION OF ALCOHOLIC BEVERAGES IMPAIRS YOUR ABILITY TO DRIVE A CAR OR OPERATE MACHINERY, AND MAY CAUSE HEALTH PROBLEMS.

DISTILLED & BOTTLED BY
CEDAR RIDGE DISTILLERY
CEDAR RAPIDS, IOWA

8 59824 00130 0

www.crdistillery.com

**IA 5¢ REFUND**

Southern West Virginia's first distillery
founded in 2002 by Rodney Facemire.

PRODUCED AND BOTTLED BY
KIRKWOOD, LTD.
SUMMERSVILLE, WEST VIRGINIA
(304) 872-7332

GOVERNMENT WARNING: (1) ACCORDING TO THE SURGEON GENERAL, WOMEN SHOULD NOT DRINK ALCOHOLIC BEVERAGES DURING PREGNANCY BECAUSE OF THE RISK OF BIRTH DEFECTS, (2) CONSUMPTION OF ALCOHOLIC BEVERAGES IMPAIRS YOUR ABILITY TO DRIVE A CAR OR OPERATE MACHINERY, AND MAY CAUSE HEALTH PROBLEMS.

# Isaiah Morgan

*RYE WHISKEY*

DISTILLERY

40% ALCOHOL BY VOLUME (80 PROOF)

7 58920 26652 4

JOURNEY MAN
DISTILLERY

RAVENSWOOD RYE

*Handmade Organic Rye Whiskey*

DISTILLED IN CHICAGO
BOTTLED AT THE
HISTORIC FEATHERBONE FACTORY
IN THREE OAKS, MI.

*375ml*

*43% Alcohol By Volume (86 Proof)*

XX
PINCHGUT HOLLOW
DISTILLERY
BUCKWHEAT
MOON
H F
WEST VIRGINIA
POTSTILL SPIRITS
BARREL AGED 30 DAYS
HAND-CRAFTED
WITH
HOMEGROWN GRAIN
(100 PROOF) 50% ALC./VOL.

750ML

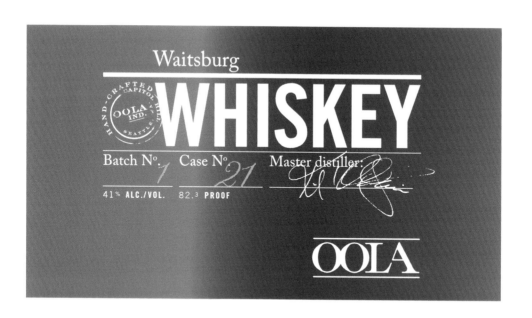

Waitsburg

# WHISKEY

Batch Nº. 1   Case Nº 21   Master distiller:

41% ALC./VOL.   82.3 PROOF

## OOLA

## MOYLAN'S

# American Single-Malt Whisky

FINISHED IN ORANGE BRANDY BARRELS
SMALL-BATCH COPPER DISTILLED
FROM 100% MALT

43% ALC./ VOL. / 86 PROOF / 750ML

STILLWATER
PETALUMA  CALIFORNIA

SPIRITS

TO CREATE THIS EXCEPTIONAL WHISKY,
MOYLAN'S DISTILLING COMPANY FIRST
FERMENTS 100% TWO-ROW BARLEY AND WHEAT,
THEN RELEASES THE SPIRIT IN A COPPER
POT STILL TO HANDCRAFT A WHISKY OF
UNCOMPROMISED QUALITY. AGED IN 100% AMERICAN
WHITE OAK BOURBON AND BEER BARRELS.

BY FINISHING IN ORANGE BRANDY BARRELS,
OUR SINGLE MALT WHISKY NEGOTIATES
A DELICATE SYMBIOSIS OF FLORAL AROMA
WITH CANDIED CITRUS FRUIT. A PLUMP,
MOUTH-WATERING BARLEY SWEETNESS ANCHORS
OUR VERSION OF THE NEW AMERICAN STANDARD.
SMALL BATCH SIZES ASSURE OUR
COMMITTMENT TO FLAVOR AND QUALITY.

WWW.STILLWATERSPIRITS.COM
WWW.MOYLANSDISTILLING.COM
STILLWATERSPIRITS@GMAIL.COM

DISTILLED AND BOTTLED BY
MOYLAN'S DISTILLING COMPANY
PETALUMA, CALIFORNIA

GOVERNMENT WARNING: (1)ACCORDING TO THE SURGEON GENERAL, WOMEN SHOULD NOT DRINK ALCOHOLIC BEVERAGES DURING PREGNANCY BECAUSE OF THE RISK OF BIRTH DEFECTS. (2)CONSUMPTION OF ALCOHOLIC BEVERAGES IMPAIRS YOUR ABILITY TO DRIVE A CAR OR OPERATE MACHINERY, AND MAY CAUSE HEALTH PROBLEMS.

A full flavored complex American Whiskey made with cherry wood smoked malt and aged in Midwest made oak barrels in our cellars.

Cheers! visit us at www.SquareOneBrewery.com!

ARTISAN SPIRITS

*Small Batch Handcrafted*

*Spirits of St. Louis*

*Made in the United States*

ARTISAN SPIRITS

*Lafayette Square*
St. Louis, Missouri

*Lafayette Square*
St. Louis, Missouri

## J.J. Neukomm

### MISSOURI MALT WHISKEY

MADE WITH CHERRY WOOD SMOKED MALT

*Single Barrel*

## Spirits of St. Louis

45% ALC./VOL. (90 PROOF)

*Small Batch Handcrafted*
ARTISAN SPIRITS

*Made in the United States*
ARTISAN SPIRITS

750ml

GOVERNMENT WARNING: (1) ACCORDING TO THE SURGEON GENERAL, WOMEN SHOULD NOT DRINK ALCOHOLIC BEVERAGES DURING PREGNANCY BECAUSE OF THE RISK OF BIRTH DEFECTS. (2) CONSUMPTION OF ALCOHOLIC BEVERAGES IMPAIRS YOUR ABILITY TO DRIVE A CAR OR OPERATE MACHINERY, AND MAY CAUSE HEALTH PROBLEMS.

DISTILLED AND BOTTLED BY SQUARE ONE BREWERY AND DISTILLERY - ST. LOUIS, MO.

Genuine
Small Batch

## Dad's Hat™

### PENNSYLVANIA RYE

WHISKEY

Using only natural, local ingredients and the most careful methods, Dad's Hat is made in Pennsylvania — the birthplace of Rye Whiskey — in honor of that wonderful, optimistic time in America's history when we made things and took care to make them well.

Dad's Hat Rye Whiskey reflects that same simple, uniquely American personality better than any other whiskey. Crisp. Unfussy. Smooth. Delicious; not lingering or heavy-handed in its finish. Perfect for every occasion. After tasting Dad's Hat, we hope that you feel the same.

45% ALC/VOL     90 PROOF     750 ML

GOVERNMENT WARNING: (1) ACCORDING TO THE SURGEON GENERAL, WOMEN SHOULD NOT DRINK ALCOHOLIC BEVERAGES DURING PREGNANCY BECAUSE OF THE RISK OF BIRTH DEFECTS. (2) CONSUMPTION OF ALCOHOLIC BEVERAGES IMPAIRS YOUR ABILITY TO DRIVE A CAR OR OPERATE MACHINERY, AND MAY CAUSE HEALTH PROBLEMS.

DISTILLED AND BOTTLED BY MOUNTAIN LAUREL SPIRITS, LLC AT THE GRUNDY MILL DISTILLERY IN BRISTOL, PA

# OTHER
# SPIRITS

OGDEN'S OWN DISTILLERY
750 ML

HANDCRAFTED HERBAL SPIRIT
40% ALC/VOL.(80 PROOF)
GRAIN NEUTRAL SPIRITS WITH NATURAL FLAVORS
GUARANA, GINSENG AND CARAMEL COLOR

DOLMEN DISTILLERY

# WORKER BEE

HONEY SPIRITS

ALCOHOL 40% BY VOLUME
··· 80 PROOF ···

375 ML

GOVERNMENT WARNING: (1) ACCORDING TO THE SURGEON GENERAL, WOMEN SHOULD NOT DRINK ALCOHOLIC BEVERAGES DURING PREGNANCY BECAUSE OF THE RISK OF BIRTH DEFECTS. (2) CONSUMPTION OF ALCOHOLIC BEVERAGES IMPAIRS YOUR ABILITY TO DRIVE A CAR OR OPERATE MACHINERY, AND MAY CAUSE HEALTH PROBLEMS.

DISTILLED AND BOTTLED BY DOLMEN DISTILLERY
McMINNVILLE, OREGON

THIS HANDCRAFTED SPIRIT BEGINS WITH HONEY PRODUCED BY MANY THOUSANDS OF HARDWORKING LOCAL BEES. I FERMENT THE HONEY INTO MEAD, OR HONEY WINE, THEN DISTILL IT IN SMALL BATCHES. AND, THOUGH THIS BOTTLE CONTAINS THE PRESENCE OF APPROXIMATELY 2.4 POUNDS OF HONEY, MY AIM IS TO CREATE A UNIQUE SPIRIT THAT CAPTURES THE ESSENTIAL FLAVOR OF THE HONEY AND ONLY A LITTLE OF THE SWEETNESS.

PRODUCT OF YAMHILL COUNTY, OR

CROP YEAR

# GREAT LAKES DISTILLERY

# PUMPKIN

SEASONAL SPIRIT

Bottle No.

SPIRITS DISTILLED FROM GRAIN & PUMPKIN
WITH SPICES AND NATURAL FLAVOR.
45% ALC. BY VOL. (90 PROOF)

WHAT DO YOU GET WHEN YOU COMBINE THE CRAFTSMANSHIP OF WISCONSIN'S FIRST SMALL BATCH DISTILLERY AND LAKEFRONT BREWERY'S AWARD WINNING SEASONAL PUMPKIN SPICE LAGER? GREAT LAKES SEASONAL PUMPKIN SPIRIT!

A LIMITED EDITION SPIRIT, WE CAREFULLY DISTILL THE ESSENCE FROM THE BEER THEN AGE IT IN OAK BARRELS UNTIL IT HAS JUST THE RIGHT COMBINATION OF PUMPKIN, SPICE, MALT AND OAKY SMOOTHNESS.

GLD
GREAT LAKES DISTILLERY

LAKEFRONT
BREWERY, INC.

WWW.GREATLAKESDISTILLERY.COM

GOVERNMENT WARNING: (1) ACCORDING TO THE SURGEON GENERAL, WOMEN SHOULD NOT DRINK ALCOHOLIC BEVERAGES DURING PREGNANCY BECAUSE OF THE RISK OF BIRTH DEFECTS. (2) CONSUMPTION OF ALCOHOLIC BEVERAGES IMPAIRS YOUR ABILITY TO DRIVE A CAR OR OPERATE MACHINERY, AND MAY CAUSE HEALTH PROBLEMS.

DISTILLED AND BOTTLED BY GREAT LAKES DISTILLERY MILWAUKEE, WI  750ML

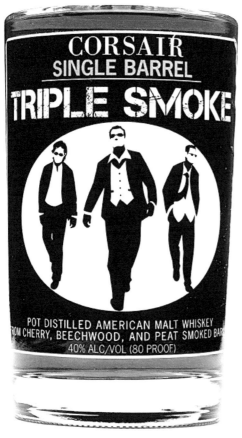

LION'S PRIDE

ORGANIC WHISKEY

DARK SPELT

SINGLE BARREL

DISTILLED FROM 100% SPELT

Made in Chicago

40% Alc. by Vol. (80 Proof)

750ml

AEppel Treow Spirits

BROWN DOG

Spirits Distilled From Sorghum
Aged with Oak, Chestnut, Apple &
and Cherry Woodchips
40% Alc. By Vol. (80 Proof)

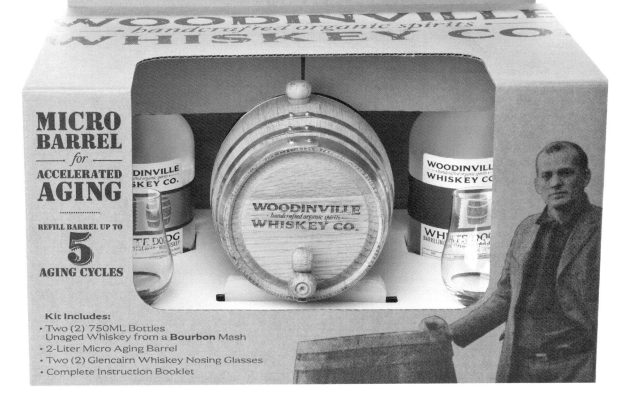

# AGE YOUR OWN
*whiskey kit*

WOODINVILLE
*handcrafted organic spirits*
WHISKEY CO.

## MICRO BARREL
*for*
## ACCELERATED AGING

REFILL BARREL UP TO

## 5
## AGING CYCLES

**Kit Includes:**
• Two (2) 750ML Bottles
  Unaged Whiskey from a **Bourbon** Mash
• 2-Liter Micro Aging Barrel
• Two (2) Glencairn Whiskey Nosing Glasses
• Complete Instruction Booklet

WOODINVILLE
WHISKEY CO.
*handcrafted organic spirits*

# CANADIAN
# SPIRITS

SCHRAMM
*Vodka*

Small Batch Organic Potato Vodka

Handcrafted & Bottled in the
Pemberton Valley, BC, Canada

750mL    40% alc./vol.

STILL WATERS

SINGLE MALT
VODKA

HAND CRAFTED BY
ARTISAN DISTILLERS
IN CANADA

40% alc./vol.    750 ml

SILVER LAKE

PREMIUM

QUADRUPLE DISTILLED

Crafted in Canada

*Johnny Ziegler*

36% alc./vol. - 750 ml

*Fruit* **Brandy** *de Fruits*

5 years aged in oak

*Winegarden Estate Ltd.*
Route 970, Baie Verte, N.B. E4M 1Z7

Product of 6
Produit du
New Brunswick

**+472597**

0408

Return
Refund
Consigne

*Johnny Ziegler*

**EAU DE VIE**

40% alc./vol. - 750 ml

*Apple* *aux Pomme* **Schnaps** *Dry*
*Black Forest Style*

*Winegarden Estate Ltd.*
Route 970, Baie Verte, N.B. E4M 1Z7

Return
Refund
Consigne

**+297960**

Product of
Produit du
New Brunswick

0407

*Johnny Ziegler*

*Fruit Brandy de Fruits*

**Senior**

36% alc./vol.    750 ml

aged in oak 10 years

*Winegarden Estate Ltd.*
Route 970, Baie Verte, N.B. E4M 1Z7

Product of
Produit du
New Brunswick

**+814825**

0407

Return
Refund
Consigne

OAKEN GIN

HANDMADE
POT-DISTILLED
AGED IN OAK

VICTORIA HAS MATURED

375 ml    45% alc./vol.

# INDEX OF DISTILLERS

# INDEX OF DISTILLERS

CPSIA information can be obtained
at www.ICGtesting.com
Printed in the USA
253709LV00001B